I0797346

Electronics
FAITH WOODLAND
LIGHTBOX
openlightbox.com

Lightbox is an all-inclusive digital solution for the teaching and learning of curriculum topics in an original, groundbreaking way. Lightbox is based on National Curriculum Standards.

STANDARD FEATURES OF LIGHTBOX

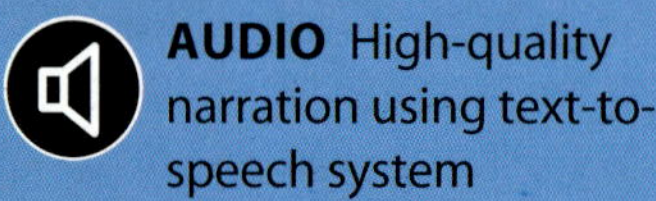

AUDIO High-quality narration using text-to-speech system

ACTIVITIES Printable PDFs that can be emailed and graded

SLIDESHOWS Pictorial overviews of key concepts

VIDEOS Embedded high-definition video clips

WEBLINKS Curated links to external, child-safe resources

TRANSPARENCIES Step-by-step layering of maps, diagrams, charts, and timelines

INTERACTIVE MAPS Interactive maps and aerial satellite imagery

QUIZZES Ten multiple choice questions that are automatically graded and emailed for teacher assessment

KEY WORDS Matching key concepts to their definitions

CONTENTS

Electronics in the United States

Americans depend on electronic devices for learning, working, communicating, and even playing.

It is hard to imagine a world without all the electronics people now use each day. From the moment they wake up to the time they go to sleep, people are in contact with electronic devices.

84 percent of **Americans** use the **internet**.

Silicon makes up **27 percent** of Earth's crust. It is used in many **electronic devices**.

The U.S. computer and **electronics industry** employs **16 percent** of all U.S. engineers, more than any other industry.

Digital alarm clocks wake people in the morning. A **global positioning system (GPS)** gets them to appointments. Students and office workers sit in front of computers. Cell phones keep people connected to one another, and televisions entertain them. Electronics is one of the United States' most important industries.

The electronics industry includes the development, production, and assembly of computers, printers, monitors, storage devices, communications equipment, and **audio** and video equipment. New processes have made such devices faster, smaller, and more powerful.

Electronic devices have **components** that control the flow of electric currents to process information. Early devices included **transistors** for sending messages. Later, tools were developed for capturing visual information with **satellite** technology. Such advances have been adapted to uses in everyday life.

Electronics Then and Now

As the United States developed and grew into a country, the electronics industry grew along with it. While early Americans did all their tasks manually, the **Industrial Revolution** gave way to the electronic age. Electronics changed the way people perform many tasks.

Talking on the Phone

The first telephones were shared lines that connected entire communities through wires attached to poles. Today, people have cell phones to speak privately to others without wires.

Sending Messages

In the 1800s, it took weeks for a letter to reach its destination. Later, messages called **telegrams** were sent using a **telegraph** machine. Now, people can send instant texts or emails electronically.

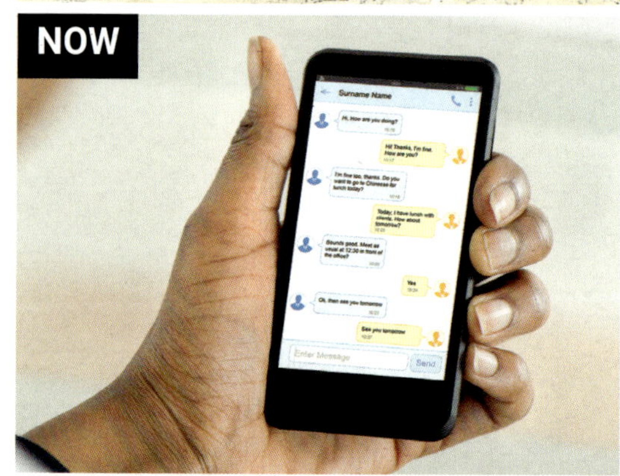

The invention of the computer in the late twentieth century affected many industries. Today, computers are integrated into products of all kinds. Computers help to make cars, appliances, and even toys function. Computers allow people to access information of all kinds and serve as a tool for storing, sending, and creating more information.

Entertainment

In the early 1900s, the invention of the radio let people listen to broadcasts and hear the latest news. Now, people enjoy live-streamed movies, music, and news on phones, TVs, or computers.

Finding Our Way

In the 1800s and 1900s, travelers used printed maps to find their way. Now, people have GPS systems that use satellite images and electronic technology to give exact directions to anywhere in the world.

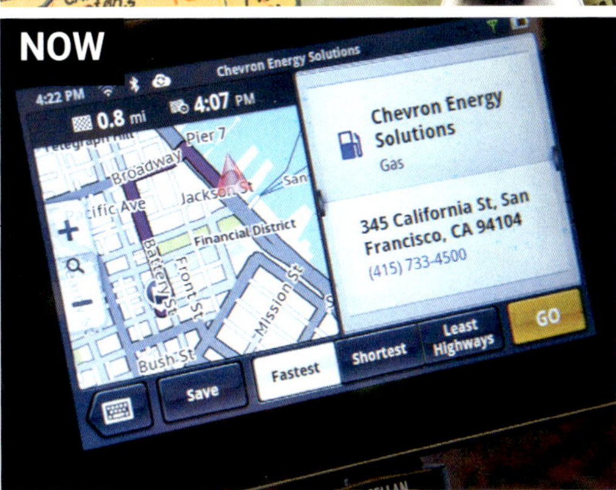

Electronics Manufacturing in the United States

Much modern electronic technology was developed in the United States. Head offices of large electronics companies are located in various states, usually in a state that has a technical research university. Technical universities teach electronic **engineering** and develop new technology.

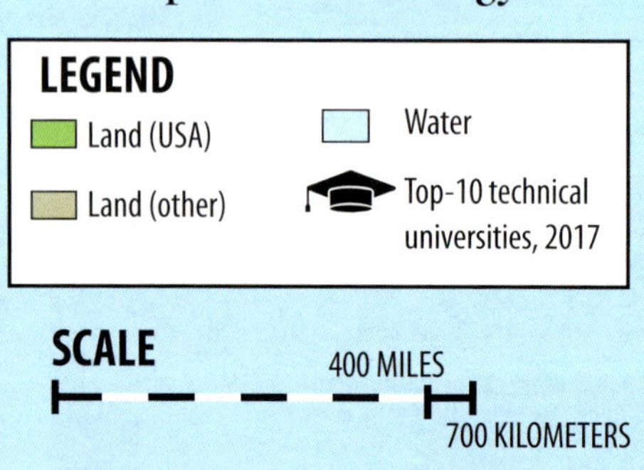

SCALE
400 MILES
700 KILOMETERS

1 Silicon Valley
California

California is home to "Silicon Valley." This area near San Francisco has the highest concentration of computer companies. Companies based there include Apple and Hewlett Packard.

2 Dallas
Texas

Texas has 8 percent of all electronic industry jobs. The state **manufactures** more than $26 billion worth of electronics every year. Dallas is home to Texas Instruments, an electronic manufacturer.

3 Cambridge Massachusetts

The state of Massachusetts manufactures $23 billion worth of electronics every year. It has more than 50,000 electronics jobs. The state also has leading colleges, such as Massachusetts Institute of Technology (MIT) in Cambridge.

4 Silicon Forest Oregon

Oregon is a center for electronics manufacturing in the United States. The state produces more than $13 billion worth of electronics per year. "Silicon Forest" is the nickname of a cluster of high-tech companies near Portland.

Electronic Products Ranked by Sales

The electronics industry contributes more than $200 billion to the U.S. **economy** per year. That makes up about 10.3 percent of the country's **gross domestic product (GDP)**. As new technology and adaptations continue to develop, sales will remain high. New products such as 3-D printers, health and fitness products, and **bluetooth** technology have contributed to continued sales in recent years.

Wearable devices monitor athletes' performance by measuring heart rate, blood pressure, and other functions.

As products become less expensive, the volume of sales rises because more people can afford the devices. Also, consumers make it a priority to purchase devices they feel are essential. Many adults feel that a cell phone is necessary to do their job, organize their lives, and stay connected to their community.

90 percent of American **adults** use **cell phones**.

80 percent of **Americans** use a laptop or desktop computer.

Equipping children with phones and computers helps them keep in contact with their family and friends. It also helps their education. Providing children with access to this technology is almost essential in order for them to do research, study, and complete school assignments. Many parents also feel their children are safer if they have a cell phone. These devices allow parents to keep in contact with their children so that they can help children cope with any emergencies.

For many children, smartphones and tablets are an important form of entertainment, as well as a source of news and information.

Timeline of Electronics Industry Events

Ever since the 1800s, U.S. engineers have led advances in electronics technology. Many modern devices were invented in the United States. Today, U.S. engineers work all over the world.

1845	1850	1880	1890	1900

1844. Samuel Morse uses an electrical device to send Morse code signals over a wire.

1870s to 1880s. Alexander Graham Bell invents the first telephone and founds the American Telephone and Telegraph Company (AT&T).

1906. Lee de Forest develops the triode. The device is key to radio communications. De Forest is sometimes called the "father of radio."

1982. The Commodore 64 home computer is launched. It becomes the best-selling personal computer of all time.

Future. People will control devices in their homes using **smart technology**. **Artificial intelligence** means that many jobs will be taken over by machines.

1928. The first television station in the United States starts broadcasting.

1985. Microsoft creates the Windows operating system. It makes personal computers far easier to use.

1930 | 1970 | 1980 | 2000 | THE FUTURE

1973. The first cell phone goes on sale.

1995. The internet becomes available for consumer use.

U.S. Electronics in the World

During the twentieth century, U.S. scientists and engineers earned a reputation for inventing and developing a wide range of electronic products. U.S. companies dominated the international market in electronics. However, people in other countries also wanted to enter the marketplace. They watched what Americans were doing, learned about U.S. products, and copied them.

In 2017, more than 40,000 students from 1,000 Chinese universities attended an electronic design contest in Beijing, China.

Starting in the 1960s, countries in Asia quickly adopted technological inventions and began manufacturing their own versions of products that had been developed in the United States. At the same time, some U.S. companies relocated their factories to Asian countries or contracted their manufacturing out to companies based there. Labor in Asia is less expensive than labor in the United States. That allows companies to build goods in Asia for a lower cost.

70 percent of all **cell phones** are produced in **CHINA**.

In **2012**, only **23 percent** of computers and electronics bought by **U.S. consumers** were made in the United States.

In the late twentieth century, China made great advances in electronics manufacturing. In 1990, China produced less than 3 percent of global manufacturing, by value, but by 2017, it produced 25 percent. Today, factories in China make many electronic components, such as transistors and **circuit boards**. They also specialize in product development and use plastic mold injection to make the bodies of electronic devices. Factories in China assemble the products as well. China also has a larger supply of qualified electronics engineers than the United States.

Despite the rise of the electronics industry in Asia, four of the world's top 10 computer and electronics companies are still located in the United States. They are Apple, Intel, Hewlett Packard, and Microsoft. Four more are located in Japan. They are Sony, Hitachi, Panasonic, and Toshiba. The remaining members of the top 10 are LG Electronics and Samsung. They are based in South Korea.

Electronics factories in China have large quality-control departments to ensure that products such as circuit boards are made to a high quality.

Facing the Issues

One crucial issue facing the United States is dealing with electronic waste. Consumers often replace their products with newer versions. This causes trash in the shape of old plastic, metal, and glass. Recycling such material effectively is a challenge.

Many electronic products are cheaper because they are produced overseas. However, this has an effect on the U.S. economy. If jobs are lost to foreign manufacturing, unemployment rises. Many people think it is better to support locally made products that create jobs for Americans and, in turn, improve the economy. At the same time, manufacturers inside the United States are increasingly using **automation**, which will result in a loss of manufacturing jobs. As part of this process, robots already do many jobs previously done by factory workers.

Old TVs, phones, and computers do not break down like organic, or living, matter. That makes them difficult to dispose of without causing pollution.

Debate

Some Americans think the country's electronics industry should manufacture its products in the United States. That would help make the country self sufficient, and help its economy grow. Should the government make it a law that all manufacturing should take place on U.S. soil?

YES

- Increased manufacturing will create more jobs for Americans.
- Students will be motivated to learn new technology and develop skills to get electronics jobs.
- The economy will grow as U.S. companies make more products and more money. Workers will have more to spend on U.S. products.

NO

- The United States is part of a global economy and should work together with other countries to make the whole world better.
- Goods and services will cost more money, so it will be harder for many people to purchase expensive items. Only rich people will be able to buy many electronic devices.

Virtual reality allows students to visit underwater archaeological sites and walk around ancient cities. They will eventually be able to interact with virtual people from the past.

Looking to the Future

The future of electronics is as unlimited as the imagination itself. It seems as if almost anything electronics engineers can think of might possibly become a reality. Experts expect to see new products, **applications**, and improvements appear in many different sectors.

Many advances will be related to health and fitness. From wristbands to actual pieces of clothing, "wearables" will give people instant feedback on their heart rate, blood pressure, and overall state of health. Homes will also monitor people's health. Fridges will record what types of food people eat and warn them if their diet is not healthy enough. Bathrooms will be able to test human waste for signs of disease or other health problems. If there are any problems, the bathroom will be linked to a system that can arrange a doctor's appointment. This type of "smart home" will be controlled from a device such as a phone or watch.

Virtual reality, also known as VR, is already part of the entertainment industry. It allows users to experience situations as if they are there. VR will increasingly be used for learning purposes in many fields of study. Medical students will be able to take a virtual tour inside a human body, for example. Students studying geography will be able to explore a real volcano.

Touch screens on watches and phones allow wearers to control devices in their homes and catch up on social media and emails while they are at work, on a day out, or on vacation.

Careers in Electronics

A career in the electronics industry is a good choice for people who are interested in the latest technology. Those who like to work creatively and invent new products would be suited to becoming electronics engineers. Electronics is also a great industry for gadget people who are fascinated by complex devices that are designed to solve very specific problems.

Electronics Engineer
Electronics engineers plan and design new products. They carry out research, evaluations, and testing. They need to both imagine a new product and have the practical skills to be able to build it. They work with teams or on individual projects.

Duties: Researches and designs new products

Education: A degree in electronics from a university or technical college

Interests: Electronic toys and games, tools, electrical equipment

Video Game Designer
Video game designers come up with ideas and story lines for games, and create new game scenarios. They may develop programs and gaming software. They also design characters and worlds, as well as new hardware.

Duties: Develops programs for games, tests products, and improves hardware

Education: Bachelor's degree in electronics, math, or computer studies

Interests: Video games, stories, films, adventure

Electronics Assembler
Electronics assemblers work in factory settings, putting parts together to complete products. They follow blueprints, and read layouts and designs. They may do wiring and soldering. They also test products and inspect work.

Duties: Assembles parts, and tests and inspects electronic devices

Education: High school diploma, college training, or apprenticeship training

Interests: Electronic devices, electricity, detailed hands-on work

Activity

Electrical circuits

All electronic devices depend on electric circuits. A circuit carries electricity from a power source, such as a battery. It enables the electricity to do useful jobs, such as turning on a lightbulb.

Make your own electrical circuit. You will need:

- 9-volt battery
- Five 3-inch (8-centimeter) metal twist ties
- A lightbulb
- A lightbulb socket with screws you can buy from a hardware or hobby store

Instructions

1. Screw the lightbulb into the socket.
2. Remove the paper at the ends of the twist ties. Twist two twist ties together to form a 6-inch (16-cm) twist tie. Make sure that the parts of the twist ties that touch are not covered in paper. Repeat this step with two more twist ties, so you have two longer twist ties.
3. Wrap one end of a long twist tie around a pole at the end of the battery.
4. Twist one end of the remaining short twist tie around a screw on the socket. Make sure no paper on the twist tie touches the screw. Ask an adult to help you. Twist the other end of the short twist tie around the other pole at the end of the battery.
5. Twist one end of the other long twist tie around the other screw on the lightbulb socket.
6. Holding the paper cover, touch the two loose wire ends of the twist ties together. Do not let any paper touch the wires. What happens to the lightbulb?
7. Pull apart the two loose ends of the twist ties. What happens to the lightbulb?
8. When the wires touched, they made a circuit joining the battery to the lightbulb. The light came on. When the wires did not touch, the light went out again. The circuit was broken.

Quiz

Check out how much you have learned about the electronics industry in the United States. The answers to all these questions are in this book.

ONE
How much of Earth's crust is silicon?

TWO
What percentage of Americans use the internet?

THREE
Which device used Morse code?

FOUR
Where is Silicon Valley?

FIVE
How much does the electronics industry contribute to the U.S. economy each year?

SIX
Who is referred to as the father of radio?

SEVEN
What percentage of cell phones are manufactured in China?

EIGHT
In what decade did the first home computers become available?

NINE
Who invented the first telephone?

TEN
Name four U.S. electronic companies.

ANSWERS
ONE 27 percent **TWO** 84 percent **THREE** The telegraph **FOUR** California **FIVE** More than $200 billion **SIX** Lee de Forest **SEVEN** 70 percent **EIGHT** 1980s **NINE** Alexander Graham Bell **TEN** Apple, Hewlett Packard, Intel, Microsoft

Key Words

applications: computer programs that allow users to perform tasks easily

artificial intelligence: computer systems that can perform tasks that normally require human characteristics such as thought, speech, or sight

audio: sound that is recorded and transmitted

automation: carried out by machines

bluetooth: a way of connecting electronic devices without wires

circuit boards: parts of a device holding many electronic components

components: parts of whole

economy: the wealth or resources of a country or region

engineering: the design and building of engines, machines, and structures

global positioning system (GPS): radio navigation system

gross domestic product (GDP): the total value of goods and services produced by a country in a year

Industrial Revolution: a period in the 1800s when many factories were built

manufactures: makes something on a large scale using machinery

satellite: an artificial body placed in orbit around Earth to collect information

smart technology: electronic devices that use sensors to adapt to their environment

telegrams: messages sent over wires by telegraph

telegraph: a system for transmitting messages along a wire

transistors: semiconductor devices with three connections

virtual reality: the computer-generated simulation of a three-dimensional image

Index

LIGHTBOX

SUPPLEMENTARY RESOURCES

Click on the plus icon found in the bottom left corner of each spread to open additional teacher resources.

- Download and print the book's quizzes and activities
- Access curriculum correlations
- Explore additional web applications that enhance the Lightbox experience

LIGHTBOX DIGITAL TITLES
Packed full of integrated media

VIDEOS

INTERACTIVE MAPS

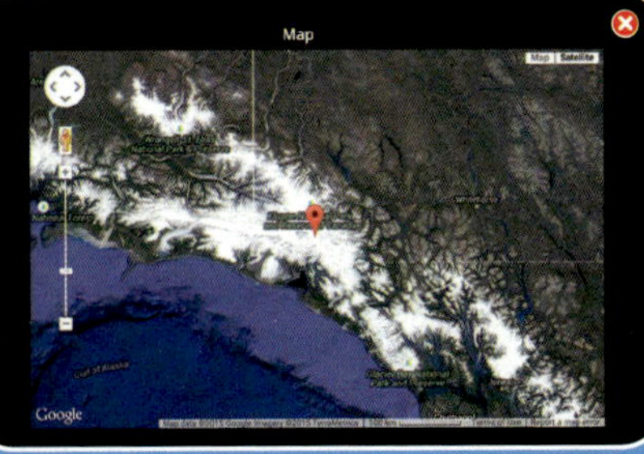

WEBLINKS

SLIDESHOWS

QUIZZES

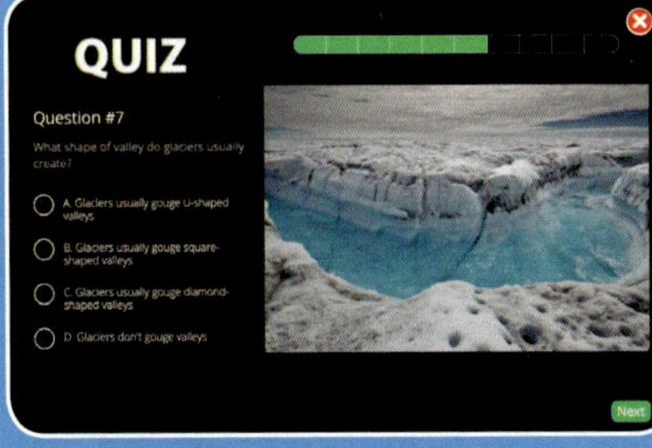

OPTIMIZED FOR

- ✔ TABLETS
- ✔ WHITEBOARDS
- ✔ COMPUTERS
- ✔ AND MUCH MORE!

Published by Smartbook Media Inc.
350 5th Avenue, 59th Floor New York, NY 10118
Website: www.openlightbox.com

Project Coordinator: Heather Kissock
Art Director: Terry Paulhus

Library of Congress Cataloging-in-Publication Data
Names: Woodland, Faith, author.
Title: Electronics / Faith Woodland.
Description: New York, NY : Smartbook Media Inc., [2019] | Series: American industries | Includes index.
Identifiers: LCCN 2017055660 (print) | LCCN 2017058125 (ebook) | ISBN 9781510535619 (Multi User ebook) | ISBN 9781510535602 (hardcover : alk. paper)
Subjects: LCSH: Electronic industries--United States--History--Juvenile literature.
Classification: LCC HD9696.U52 (ebook) | LCC HD9696.U52 W66 2019 (print) | DDC 338.4/76213810973--dc23
LC record available at https://lccn.loc.gov/2017055660

Printed in Brainerd, Minnesota, United States
1 2 3 4 5 6 7 8 9 0 22 21 20 19 18

042018
120517

Every reasonable effort has been made to trace ownership and to obtain permission to reprint copyright material. The publisher would be pleased to have any errors or omissions brought to its attention so that they may be corrected in subsequent printings.
The publisher acknowledges Getty Images, Alamy, Newscom, Shutterstock, and iStock as its primary image suppliers for this title.